A+ books

Bilingual Picture Dictionaries

My First Book of

German Words

by Katy R. Kudela

Translator: Translations.com

apple
der Apfel
(AP-fel)

Capstone press

Mankato, Minnesota

Table of Contents

How to Use This Dictionary

This book is full of useful words in both German and English. The English word appears first, followed by the German word. Look below each German word for help to sound it out. Try reading the words aloud.

Topic Heading in English

English: **body**

German: **der Körper** (CURR-per)

hair
die Haare
(HAH-ruh)

head
der Kopf
(kopf)

ear
das Ohr
(ohr)

eye
das Auge
(OU-guh)

nose
die Nase
(NAH-zuh)

mouth
der Mund
(moont)

leg
das Bein
(bain)

arm
der Arm
(arm)

hand
die Hand
(hant)

foot
der Fuß
(foos)

6

7

Topic Heading in German

Word in English
Word in German
(pronunciation)

Notes about the German Language

The German language uses two dots above the vowels a, o, and u. This umlaut gives these vowels a different sound.

ä (eh)   ö (er)   ü (ee)

In German, the symbol ß is used. This symbol has an "ss" sound.

Germans usually include "der," "die," and "das" before nouns. These all mean "the" in German. The pronunciations for these articles are below.

der (dare)   **die** (dee)   **das** (dahs)

uncle
der Onkel
(OHN-kel)

mother
die Mutter
(MUHT-er)

cousin
der Vetter
(FET-er)

aunt
die Tante
(TAHN-te)

baby
das Baby
(BEH-bee)

4

German: # die Familie (fah-MEE-lee-uh)

grandmother
die Großmutter
(GROHS-muht-er)

father
der Vater
(FAHT-er)

grandfather
der Großvater
(GROHS-faht-er)

sister
die Schwester
(SHVES-ter)

brother
der Bruder
(BROOD-er)

hair
die Haare
(HAH-ruh)

head
der Kopf
(kopf)

ear
das Ohr
(ohr)

eye
das Auge
(OU-guh)

nose
die Nase
(NAH-zuh)

mouth
der Mund
(moont)

arm
der Arm
(arm)

hand
die Hand
(hant)

German: der Körper (CURR-per)

leg
das Bein
(bain)
foot
der Fuß
(foos)

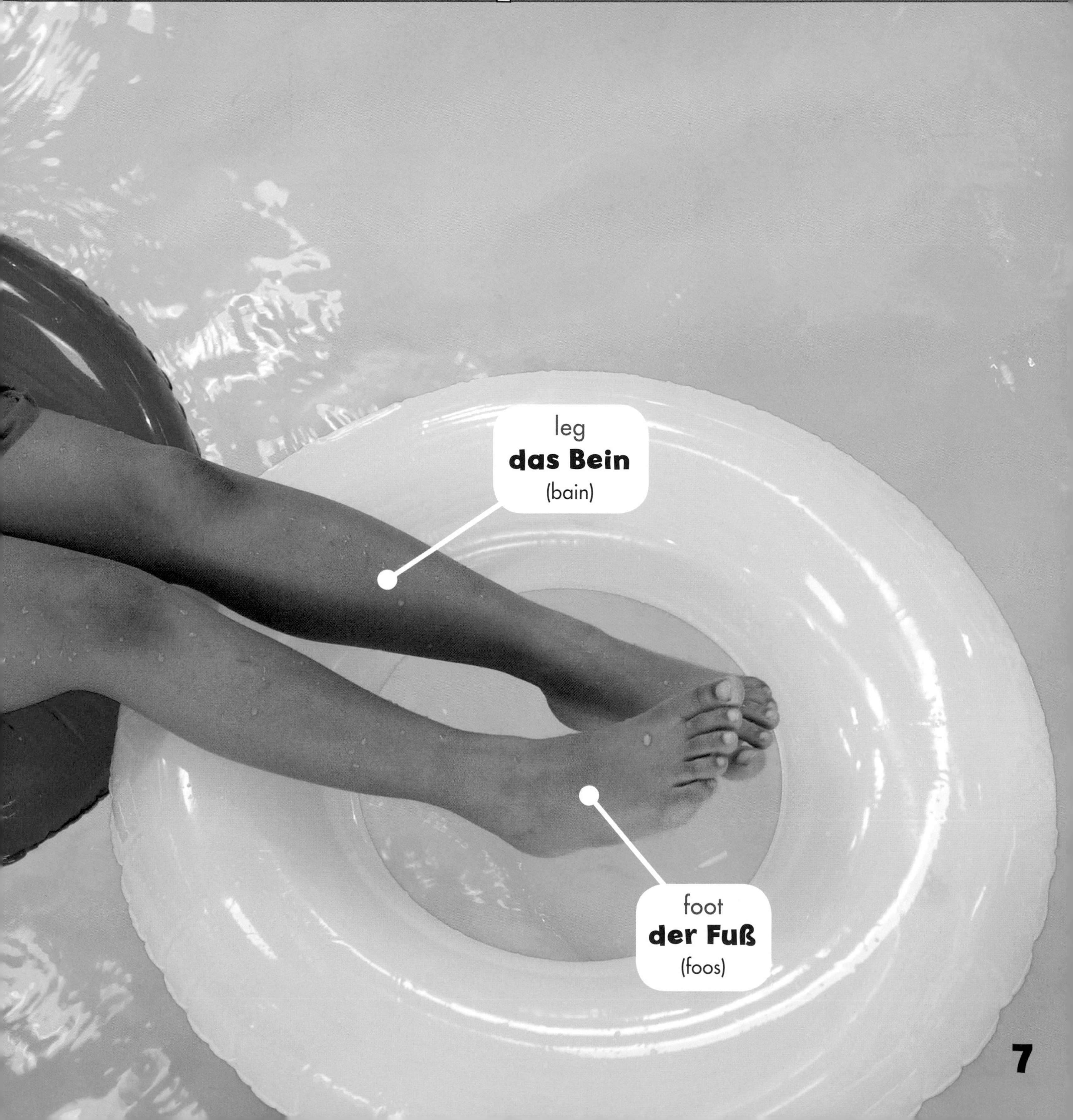

coat
die Jacke
(YAK-kuh)

pajamas
der Schlafanzug
(SHLAF-an-tsook)

shorts
die kurzen Hosen
(KOOR-tsuh HOH-zuhn)

boot
der Stiefel
(SHTEE-fel)

8

shoe
der Schuh
(shoo)

hat
die Mütze
(MEE-tsuh)

pants
die Hose
(HOH-zuh)

sock
die Socke
(ZOCK-kuh)

dress
das Kleid
(klait)

shirt
das Hemd
(hemt)

9

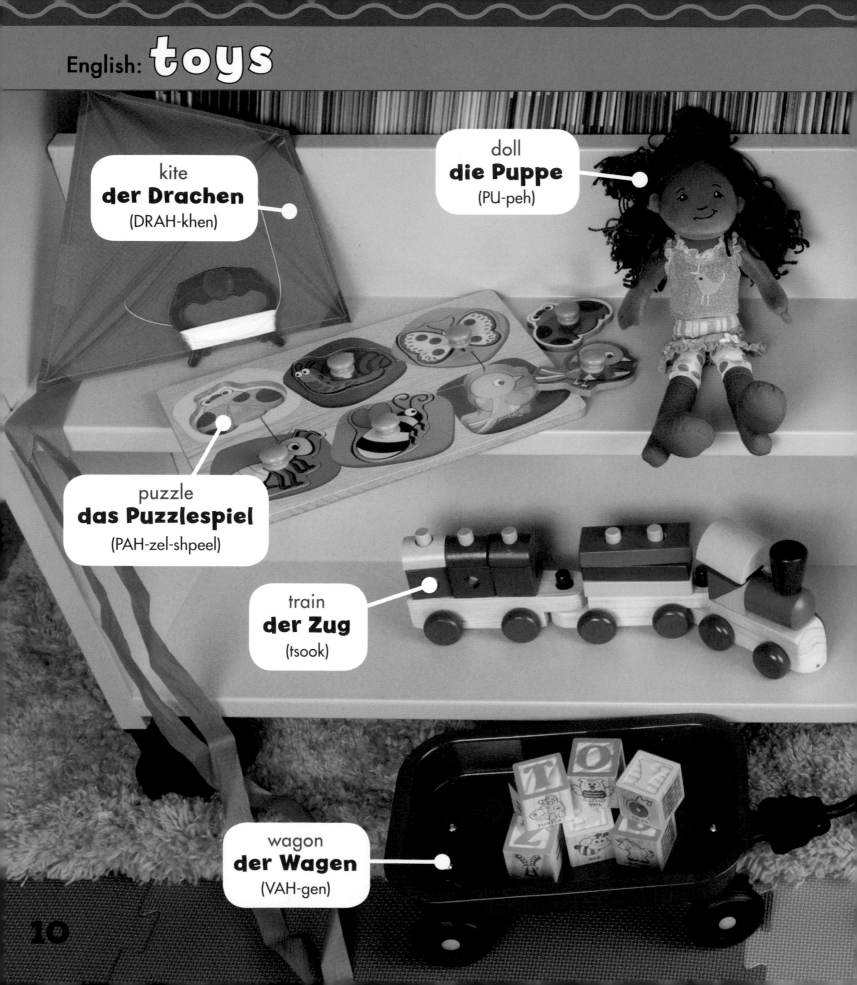

kite
der Drachen
(DRAH-khen)

doll
die Puppe
(PU-peh)

puzzle
das Puzzlespiel
(PAH-zel-shpeel)

train
der Zug
(tsook)

wagon
der Wagen
(VAH-gen)

puppet
die Handpuppe
(HANT-pup-puh)

skateboard
das Skateboard
(SKET-bohrd)

jump rope
das Springseil
(SHPRING-zail)

ball
der Ball
(bal)

bat
der Schläger
(SHLEH-ger)

window
das Fenster
(FENS-ter)

picture
das Bild
(bilt)

lamp
die Lampe
(LAM-puh)

dresser
der Schrank
(shrank)

curtain
der Vorhang
(FOHR-hang)

blanket
die Decke
(DECK-kuh)

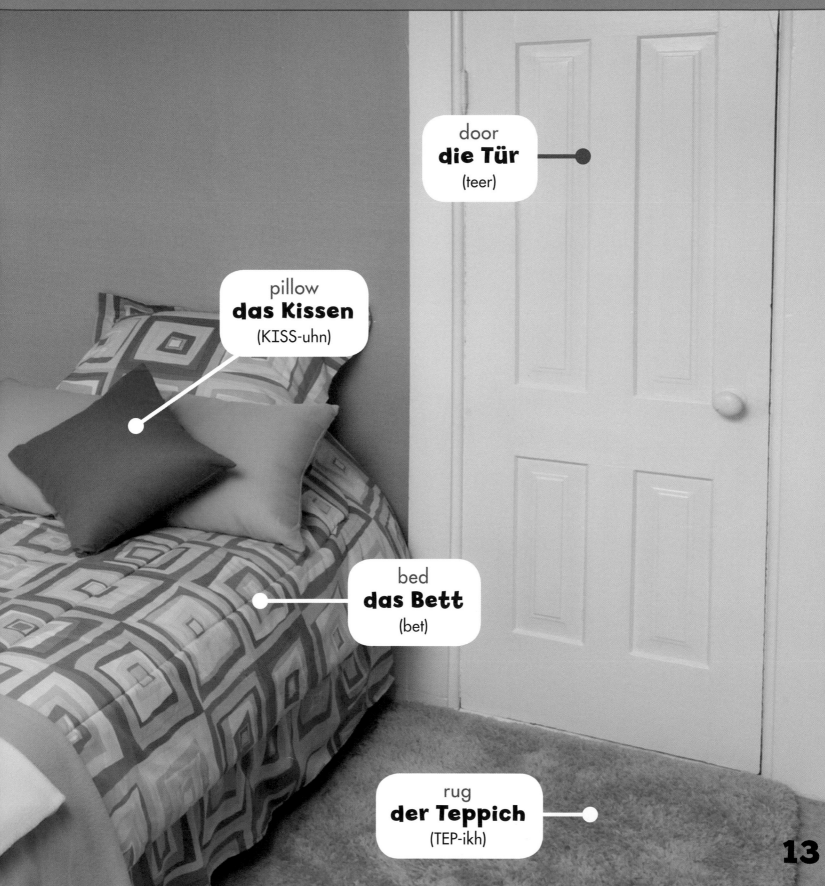

door
die Tür
(teer)

pillow
das Kissen
(KISS-uhn)

bed
das Bett
(bet)

rug
der Teppich
(TEP-ikh)

bathtub
die Badewanne
(BAH-duh-van-nuh)

soap
die Seife
(ZAIF-uh)

toilet
die Toilette
(TOY-let-tuh)

German: das Badezimmer (BAH-de-tsim-mer)

mirror
der Spiegel
(SHPEE-gel)

toothbrush
die Zahnbürste
(TSAHN-beer-stuh)

toothpaste
die Zahnpasta
(TSAHN-pas-tah)

comb
der Kamm
(kam)

sink
das Waschbecken
(VAHSH-beck-en)

towel
das Handtuch
(HANT-tookh)

brush
die Bürste
(BEER-stuh)

pot
der Topf
(topf)

stove
der Herd
(hairt)

bowl
die Schüssel
(SHEES-sel)

oven
der Backofen
(BACK-oh-fen)

refrigerator
der Kühlschrank
(KEEL-shrank)

knife
das Messer
(MESS-er)

table
der Tisch
(tish)

spoon
der Löffel
(LUHF-fel)

plate
der Teller
(TELL-er)

fork
die Gabel
(GAH-bel)

milk
die Milch
(milkh)

carrot
die Karotte
(kah-ROH-teh)

bread
das Brot
(broht)

apple
der Apfel
(AP-fel)

butter
die Butter
(BOOT-er)

egg
das Ei
(eye)

pea
die Erbse
(AIRB-seh)

orange
die Orange
(or-AHN-shuh)

sandwich
das Sandwich
(SEN-witch)

rice
der Reis
(raiss)

19

tractor
der Traktor
(TRAC-tohr)

hay
das Heu
(hoy)

fence
der Zaun
(tsown)

farmer
der Bauer
(BOW-er)

sheep
das Schaf
(shaf)

pig
das Schwein
(shvain)

20

leaf
das Blatt
(blat)

butterfly
der Schmetterling
(SHMET-er-ling)

flower
die Blume
(BLOO-muh)

shovel
die Schaufel
(SHOW-fel)

bird
der Vogel
(FOH-gull)

worm
der Wurm
(voorm)

German: **der Garten** (GAHR-ten)

plant
die Pflanze
(PFLAN-tsuh)

grass
das Gras
(grahs)

dirt
die Erde
(AIR-duh)

seed
der Samen
(ZAH-men)

23

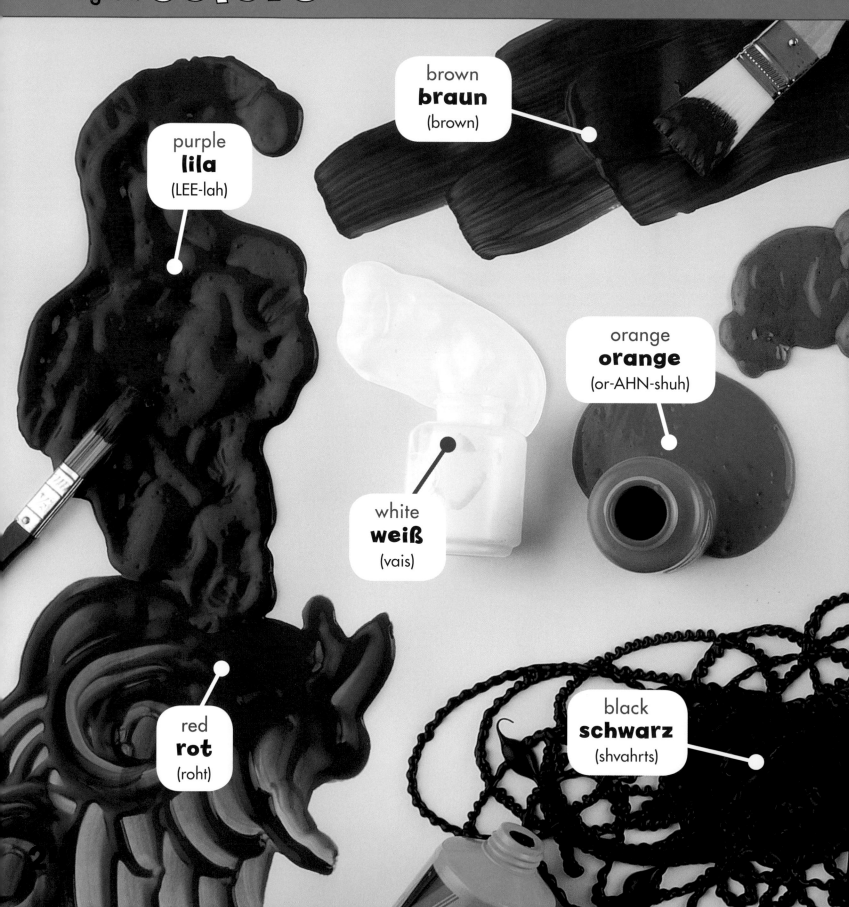

brown
braun
(brown)

purple
lila
(LEE-lah)

orange
orange
(or-AHN-shuh)

white
weiß
(vais)

red
rot
(roht)

black
schwarz
(shvahrts)

pink
rosa
(ROH-zah)

blue
blau
(blow)

yellow
gelb
(gelp)

green
grün
(green)

25

teacher
die Lehrerin
(LAY-ruh-rin)

book
das Buch
(bookh)

crayon
der Buntstift
(BUNT-shtift)

desk
der Schreibtisch
(SHRIBE-tish)

pencil
der Bleistift
(BLY-shtift)

map
die Landkarte
(LANT-kahr-tuh)

clock
die Uhr
(oor)

computer
der Computer
(KOHM-pyu-ter)

chair
der Stuhl
(shtool)

paper
das Papier
(pah-PEER)

27

traffic light
die Ampel
(AM-pel)

library
die Bücherei
(BEE-khuh-rye)

store
das Geschäft
(guh-SHEFT)

bicycle
das Fahrrad
(FAHR-rat)

car
das Auto
(OW-toh)

28

tree
der Baum
(bowm)

bus
der Bus
(boos)

park
der Park
(pahrk)

street
die Straße
(SHTRAH-suh)

sign
das Schild
(shilt)

STOP

29

Numbers • **die Zahlen** (TSAH-len)

1. one • **eins** (ains)
2. two • **zwei** (tsvai)
3. three • **drei** (drai)
4. four • **vier** (feer)
5. five • **fünf** (feenf)

6. six • **sechs** (zekhs)
7. seven • **sieben** (ZEE-ben)
8. eight • **acht** (ahkht)
9. nine • **neun** (noyn)
10. ten • **zehn** (tsayn)

Useful Phrases • **Nützliche Wörter** (NEETS-li-khuh VUR-ter)

yes • **ja** (yah)

no • **nein** (nine)

hello • **hallo** (HAL-loh)

good-bye • **auf Wiedersehen** (ouf VEE-der-zayn)

good morning • **guten Morgen** (GOOT-en MOHR-gen)

good night • **gute Nacht** (GOOT-uh nahkht)

please • **bitte** (BIT-tuh)

thank you • **danke** (DAHN-kuh)

excuse me • **Entschuldigung** (ehnt-SHUL-dih-gung)

My name is _____. • **Ich heiße** _____. (ikh HAI-ssuh)

Read More

German Picture Dictionary. Princeton, N.J.: Berlitz, 2003.

Let's Learn German Picture Dictionary. New York: McGraw-Hill, 2003.

Morris, Neil. *Oxford First German Words.* New York: Oxford University Press, 2008.

Internet Sites

FactHound offers a safe, fun way to find Internet sites related to this book. All of the sites on FactHound have been researched by our staff.

Here's all you do:

Visit *www.facthound.com*

FactHound will fetch the best sites for you!

A+ Books are published by Capstone Press,
151 Good Counsel Drive, P.O. Box 669, Mankato, Minnesota 56002.
www.capstonepub.com

Books published by Capstone Press are manufactured with paper
containing at least 10 percent post-consumer waste.

Library of Congress Cataloging in Publication Data
Kudela, Katy R.
    My first book of German words / by Katy R. Kudela.
    p. cm. — (A+ books. Bilingual picture dictionaries)
    Summary: "Simple text paired with themed photos invite the reader to learn to speak
German" — Provided by publisher.
    Includes bibliographical references.
    ISBN 978-1-4296-3296-6 (library binding)
    1. Picture dictionaries, German — Juvenile literature. 2. Picture dictionaries,
English — Juvenile literature. 3. German language — Dictionaries, Juvenile — English.
4. English language — Dictionaries, Juvenile — German. I. Title. II. Series.
PF3628.K83 2010
433'.21 — dc22   2009005516

Credits

Juliette Peters, designer; Wanda Winch, media researcher

Photo Credits

Capstone Press/Gary Sundermeyer, cover (pig), 20 (farmer with tractor, pig)
Capstone Press/Karon Dubke, cover (ball, sock), back cover (toothbrush, apple), 1, 3,
     4–5, 6–7, 8–9, 10–11, 12–13, 14–15, 16–17, 18–19, 22–23, 24–25, 26–27
Image Farm, back cover, 1, 2, 31, 32 (design elements)
iStockphoto/Andrew Gentry, 28 (main street)
Photodisc, cover (flower)
Shutterstock/Adrian Matthiassen, cover (butterfly); David Hughes, 20 (hay); Eric Isselee,
     20–21 (horse); hamurishi, 28 (bike); Jim Mills, 29 (stop sign); Kelli Westfal, 28
     (traffic light); Levgeniia Tikhonova, 21 (chickens); Margo Harrison, 20 (sheep);
     MaxPhoto, 21 (cow and calf); Melinda Fawver, 29 (bus); Robert Elias, 20–21
     (barn, fence); Vladimir Mucibabic, 28–29 (city skyline)

Note to Parents, Teachers, and Librarians

Learning to speak a second language at a young age has been shown to improve overall
academic performance, boost problem-solving ability, and foster an appreciation for other
cultures. Early exposure to language skills provides a strong foundation for other subject
areas, including math and reasoning. Introducing children to a second language can help to
lay the groundwork for future academic success and cultural awareness.

Printed in the United States of America in North Mankato, Minnesota.
112010
005993R